PLAY THE GAME

Soccer

Soccer

KEN JONES

Hamlyn

London·New York·Sydney·Toronto

Contents

pages 4/5: Argentina v Scotland, 1978
pages 62/3: Arsenal v Orient, FA Cup 1978

Acknowledgments

The author and publisher gratefully acknowledge the generous assistance of Queen's Park Rangers, Dave Clement (dark shirt) and Peter Hocker (goalkeeper). Grateful thanks also to Kim Ludlow (light shirt).
Illustrations
All the photographs in this book are by Mark Moylan/All-Sport with the exception of the following:
Don Morley/All-Sport pages 4/5;
Colorsport, London page 35; Sporting Pictures (UK) Ltd., London pages 62/3.
Diagrams: Maurice Brownfoot 1 to 5; Karel Feuerstein 6 to 9.

Published by
The Hamlyn Publishing Group Limited
London · New York · Sydney · Toronto
Astronaut House, Feltham, Middlesex, England

© Copyright The Hamlyn Publishing Group Limited 1984

Originally published as *How to play Soccer*

ISBN 0 600 34765 6

Printed in Italy

Introduction

The two essentials to success at soccer are a mastery of the basic skills and having the strength to perform these skills consistently and effectively. Actual size is less important.

Gordon McQueen, the Manchester United centre-half, is huge, his team-mate Lou Macari is tiny. They are both world-class players and were in Scotland's squad for the 1978 World Cup. The common factor is strength. Macari, pound for pound, is probably as strong as McQueen.

Pelé, perhaps the most accomplished footballer of all time, is not a big man, but at his peak he had a marvellous physique and generated immense power.

Many people felt that John Charles, a great Welsh international, was the perfect size and shape for a footballer. Charles stood 6 feet 2 inches, weighed around 14 stone (186 pounds) and could play anywhere. Some felt he was the finest centre-half in the world. Others said that he had no rivals among the great centre-forwards. But recognition of his supreme athleticism was unanimous. No player has been more beautifully built. Few struck more immediate fear into the opposition.

Strength, when applied properly, gives you power; the surge of energy needed for sprinting, jumping, turning, tackling and kicking.

Tactics and organization are also factors when chasing soccer success at the highest level. These are no substitutes for skill, but are designed to make the best use of skill.

The Brazilian manager, Claudio Coutinho, acknowledged this fact during the 1978 World Cup finals when he said 'Brazilian football is famous for flair and technique but we can no longer rely upon that alone. Our players must become more responsible, our team must be better organized.'

A largely dour Brazil beat Italy for third place and might easily have reached the Final. But Coutinho was constantly under fire accused of putting a scowl on the face of Brazilian soccer.

Argentina won the World Cup for the first time playing at a whirlwind pace, riding their luck, inspired by Mario Kempes, an outstanding striker who ran the ball disconcertingly at defenders.

Europe's teams limped home and trained observers began to catalogue conclusions. The most obvious was that a mastery of basic technique is still the biggest asset on a soccer pitch. Strength and organization, the strong points of European football of recent years, must be complemented by the ability to receive and move the ball at speed.

This book will help to teach these basic skills.

Chapter One
Fitness and Kit

Crystal Palace won the FA Youth Cup in 1977 and 1978 with a team that had struggled against stronger boys of their own age a year or so earlier. When the Cup was won for the second time, five of the Palace youngsters were appearing regularly in Second Division league football.

The Palace manager Terry Venables and his youth coach John Cartwright had been rewarded for concentrating on skill, allowing their youth players to gain strength naturally and steadily. 'We ignored the fact that strength is often a dominating factor in a certain age group' said Cartwright. 'We concentrated on technique and when the boys matured physically they were in a different class.'

Stamina, strength and speed are influential factors at any level of football and fit players will gain more enjoyment from the game. The professional has to be fit if he is to survive the rigours of a long season. On the other hand those who are not being paid, who are simply playing football for pleasure must decide what level of fitness they are aiming for.

Training at any level should be broken up accordingly into: endurance training, power and strength training, skill training.

Endurance training
The aim is to develop the efficiency of the heart and lungs so that the blood and oxygen supply to the working muscles is increased. This helps muscles to function and reduces fatigue.

Training consists of rhythmical exercises, skipping movements and running. Use other movements that are related to soccer. Stop start running. Change of pace and direction. Jumping. Kicking and dribbling.

Power and strength training
There is a need for power in soccer, that surge of energy when jumping, sprinting, turning, kicking and tackling. Strengthening exercises for all parts of the body can be used. Press-ups, pull-ups, running uphill at speed and weight and pulley exercises all serve to give a player the explosive power he will need.

The gap between professional seasons is now so small that players no longer have to endure the weeks of punishment commonplace years ago.

But full fitness must be re-established and it is essential that this is maintained throughout the season. Non-professional players, both senior and junior, usually start off with great enthusiasm and the light evenings of summer encourage them to turn up in force.

It is more difficult when the winter draws in, especially if adequate indoor facilities aren't available. But the keen player will make an effort even if it is only a run along the road.

If you are lucky enough to have a training area that can be used throughout the season then make the most of it. Organize a schedule that provides the best possible chance of being fit for the game at your level.

Kit

Some of the world's greatest players learned their skills with a worn tennis ball or even a tightly-bound bundle of rags. Urchins displaying miraculous skills on the beaches of Rio may not have the price of a decent meal but between them they have the price of a ball and so the price of a game. One of the reasons why soccer is taking root in the United States is that it is cheap to play compared to other sports.

Smart kit won't turn you into a good player, but if you look and feel the part it all helps towards being successful. The usual kit consists of a shirt, shorts, socks, shin pads and footwear.

Well-fitting boots are essential. Boots were once made of hard leather and had high backs and heavy, moulded toe-caps. They had to be softened with polish and 'broken in'. The boots expanded with use and professionals usually bought a full size smaller. It seems astonishing that players were able to reach such a high standard of touch with such heavy equipment.

There is now a vast range of boots on the market, most of them bearing names made famous by international players who are paid handsome advertising fees. Choose carefully. Professionals are provided with boots for all occasions. This is a costly business so it is better to settle for a pair that will be suited to most weather conditions. Rubber-studded boots may feel comfortable but aren't practical if the surface is not dry and grassless. Boots with screw-in studs of varying length that can be changed to suit the conditions are the best value.

Look after them – they cost enough! Let boots dry naturally but not in your bag! A good shoe polish should keep them in good condition and remember to get repairs done quickly. Many boots have nylon studs. If these are allowed to wear down they become razor sharp and dangerous.

Professional clubs often penalize players who are injured as the result of not wearing shin pads. Nevertheless players can be seen each week in First Division games with their socks rolled down around their ankles. It's a dangerous fashion in such a high-speed contact game and unfortunately it is copied. The modern shin-guard is plastic, light and comfortable and there is no excuse for not wearing them.

Look good and you will feel good, but remember that it is skill and application of that skill that counts most of all.

Chapter Two
Kicking and Shooting

Passing stretcher-bearers on the way out to play Portugal one cold, wet night in Lisbon, an England forward joked: 'They'll do me after 20 minutes out there.' Malcolm Macdonald's attitude was entirely different. 'The only way I'm coming off is shoulder high' growled the Arsenal forward. That compulsion doesn't always work for Macdonald, but it has helped him to become a prolific goalscorer in club football.

The great Hungarian team of the 1950s played numerous practice games against inferior opposition. They ran up massive totals simply to develop a goalhungry mood. Every chance should be put away in training.

Gerd Muller, the former West German World Cup star, has never looked a class player, but he turns quickly and has the great goalscorer's gift of striking the ball quickly through a short arc. Charlie George of Derby has it. So did George Best, Jimmy Greaves and Denis Law.

Ferenc Puskas, the legendary Hungarian, shot memorably from everywhere. Puskas could hit them from any angle on the volley, half-volley and at full stretch. He could swerve his shots, dip them and even make the ball kick up from the floor.

It doesn't matter how the ball is put into the net as long as it gets there legitimately. Pelé proved that when scoring well over a thousand goals for Santos, New York Cosmos and Brazil. Nevertheless, if you improve your kicking of the ball you will certainly increase the number of goals you score.

There will be few opportunities in a match for kicking a dead

Full instep kick. Note the standing foot is well up to the ball. There is a smooth backlift and follow-through.

ball so, as with all skills, once you have learned the fundamentals practise on the move. Pass on the run, shoot on the run, centre on the run.

The ball can be kicked: with the full instep; with the inside and outside of the instep; with the inside and outside of the foot; with the toe; with the heel.

It can be driven, pushed, flighted and flicked. By altering the position of the head and the standing foot, the ball can be lofted or

The full volley.

Volleying on the turn. The player is well balanced, and by leaning away from the flight of the ball he keeps it down.

Backheels often work, but remember you will be making a blind pass. Never backheel the ball close to your own goal.

kept low. For all low kicks the standing foot should be well up to the ball, but far enough to one side so that there is room for a clear swing. The head position is critical. If the head is well over the ball, the ball will keep low. If the head is up, the ball will go up.

Beginners should concentrate on kicking straight with a smooth backlift and follow-through.

The instep kick is used for shooting and long passes. The inside of the foot kick is used for short passes.

Even professionals were once satisfied if they could send the ball straight when passing or shooting. Most of them are now skilled at swerving the ball.

Modern football is fast. It is a game of instant decisions. The ball will often have to be played first time. This not only means altering the direction of the ball along the ground but also striking it in mid-air.

Some of the most spectacular goals are volleyed or half-volleyed, the combination of kicking power and ball speed producing tremendous velocity.

It is wrong to assume that good football is always played on the ground. Some of the most productive passes are sent through

Swerving the ball with the outside of the foot.

the air. Liam Brady (Arsenal and Eire) and Graham Souness (Liverpool and Scotland) are fine examples of British players who have developed the art of flighting the ball over defenders.

Backheels are made blind. Use them sparingly and never close to your own goal. Toepokes are useful in an emergency, particularly when it is impossible to get close to the ball. Acrobatic kicks are fine if they work, but are difficult to practise.

Professionals must be able to kick a long way. If they can't, their game becomes predictable. They are forced to play at short range and will struggle to make contact with team-mates who are well-positioned for a breakaway.

Power is important when shooting. Attackers should always try to be on target, but those who also strike the ball powerfully are more likely to score.

Passes driven into a crowded goalmouth may ricochet anywhere. Attackers who react quickly will often be able to snap up half-chances. Someone should always follow in on shots – the goalkeeper may fumble.

Centres crossed to the near post are a problem for goalkeepers, who must also guard against long centres. Be ready for them. Attack the ball at all times.

A dribble or a chip may work, but the goalkeeper is usually most vulnerable low down and close to his feet. This is the spot to aim for.

Imagination is priceless in front of goal, but know how other players are positioned.

If you never shoot you cannot hope to score. Long-range shooting often pays off and this became a spectacular feature of the 1978 World Cup.

Scotland, leading the Dutch 3–1 in Mendoza, were on the brink of sensationally salvaging their cause when they were broken by Johnny Rep's fierce drive from well outside the penalty area.

There was more to come, particularly from Holland. Going on to play West Germany in Cordoba, they drew 2–2 and one of their

Swerving the ball with the inside of the foot.

Lean back to get the ball
into the air.

goals was a memorable effort from the midfield player Arie Haan whose shot from fully 35 yards was struck so powerfully that Sepp Maier in the German goal was only beginning to react when the ball flew past his right shoulder.

Maier's experience was nothing compared to that of Italy's goalkeeper Dino Zoff. One of the oldest and most experienced players in the World Cup, he was to be beaten from outside the penalty area four times in four days.

The Italians were ahead 1–0 against Holland in a match that decided one of the finalists when Erny Brandts, a young defender, swung his right foot at a loose ball and drilled it past Zoff. Then came an astonishing long-range goal from Haan. He was a long way out when a free kick was pushed short into his stride. Haan ran on a few yards, took aim and Zoff was helpless as the ball flew in off the top of his left hand upright.

It was now evident that Zoff at 35 was no longer applying the exact geometry of goalkeeping, no longer leaving his line to narrow the angle. He was to pay the penalty for this again in the match for third place.

By then, the Brazilian right-back Nelinho had established a reputation for fearsome shooting, his presence at free kicks causing a surge of anticipation among the cameramen. But it was on the run and from a wide angle that he scored against Italy with a 40 yarder that boomeranged around Zoff into the top far corner. Then it was Dirceu's turn. The little Brazilian midfield player had been one of his country's few genuine successes and he finished his World Cup gloriously with a volleyed goal that destroyed Zoff again.

This orgy of power shooting excited both fans and coaches, but the most menacing finisher in the 1978 World Cup was clearly Kempes with his electrifying pace close to goal.

Great goalscorers hit the ball quickly. Remember that most chances have to be taken on the run. The ball may be bouncing, it may be in the air. It will seldom come as you would like it. Build your shooting practices accordingly. Get used to striking the ball first time.

14

Exercises

Kicking Practice This can be boring when done in pairs. Instead work in threes with one in the middle.

You can now alter the length of your kicks. Start by using the inside of the foot. Keep on the move and run to the ball. Play the ball. Move back. Move sideways. Change feet.

Think about balance. Use your arms. Get into the habit of using your body. Dummy or feint before you play the ball. Touch the ball left or right before playing it. Play the ball first time.

Play the ball in short to the man in the middle, when he returns it, kick long to the far man. He repeats the pattern.

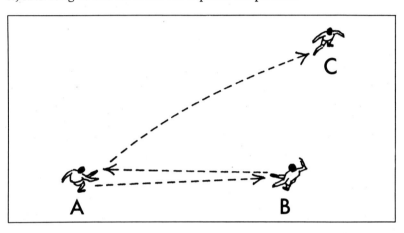

Diagram 1: A takes a return pass from B and kicks a long ball to C.

Target practice See how often you can shoot into goal from various distances and angles. Select a target. (Centre circle, penalty spot).

Mark targets on a wall. Return the rebounds first time. Do this in pairs.

Professionals must be able to kick a long way. Note the power build-up in Dave Clement's thighs.

Chapter Three
Passing

If asked to describe 'good' football most fans would talk about a short-passing game. But too much short passing leads to long periods of congestion in midfield and is often responsible for boring matches.

Passing can be accurate but negative. It can also be over-ambitious. Slow passes may never get there. Powerful passes may run out of play. If a forward pass is delayed, players may have already run offside.

The technique employed when delivering a pass is largely irrelevant. The things that matter are imagination, choice, accuracy, pace and timing.

Forwards who work hard and intelligently off the ball get discouraged if no attempt is made to find them or if the passing is untidy. Poor passing ruins teamwork and destroys confidence. A player who passes badly is making the game more difficult.

Many players with outstanding potential fall short of being top class because they consistently accept the easy way out. In contrast, Johnny Giles, an outstanding Eire star, always looks for the far man first. There have been few better examples of a creative player who consistently selects the right pass. Giles always has his head up, taking in as much of the play as possible. He not only has the courage to go for a penetrating pass but the patience to close

Side-foot passing. The body is well over the ball to keep it low. Use the inside of the foot for short passes.

the game down. He only settles for a safe pass if there is nothing else available.

Possession is important, but not always critical. Holland frequently gave the ball away when winning through to the 1974 World Cup Final against West Germany. Confidence in their ability to get the ball back quickly enabled them to adopt an exhilarating style that was overwhelmingly successful until they lost in the Final.

Good teams back up well, offering the man on the ball a variety of options. This was the essence of Nottingham Forest's football when winning the English League Championship and the Football League Cup in 1978. They kept things simple, varying the speed of their passes to change the pace of the game. They reacted quickly whenever they won the ball so that attacks were always supported in strength and at speed.

The best passes go between and behind the oncoming defenders; this puts them temporarily out of the game so providing more room for the attackers. Similarly, a 'wall pass' is used to beat a tackler. Rather than dribble past him the attacker, A, passes to a nearby team-mate, B, and runs past the defender to collect the immediate return pass. In fact, B acts like a wall off which the ball is bounced.

Wolves in their great years relied almost exclusively on long passes, believing that the more often they put the ball into the opposing penalty area, the more likely they were to score. The policy was productive while Wolves could call upon direct, speedy attackers, particularly on the wings, When these players couldn't be replaced. Wolves fell away.

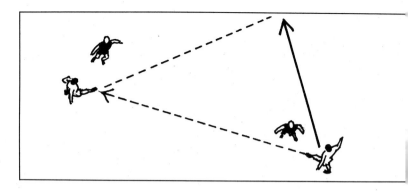

Diagram 2: The simple wall pass.

However, a constant flow of long passes may not be any more profitable than complicated short passing moves. An added disadvantage is that long passes are more likely to be intercepted. It is better to establish a balance.

Be aware of preferences. Which forwards will chase hungrily and bravely? Which of them are more comfortable and dangerous when the ball is fed to their feet?

There is more to be gained from playing the ball into a defence than across it. It is here that attackers should develop good understanding since the wall pass (also called the 'one-two' or 'give and go') used smartly on the edge of the penalty area will unnerve the best defenders.

It is essential that the ball is moved accurately out of defence although it is unwise to take chances in the penalty area. 'Never run the ball out of your own box' growled Bill Shankly, the famous former Liverpool manager, when itemizing important principles of play.

Also it isn't enough for defenders to remain in touch with the midfield players; they must also be able to find attackers who are moving to create space further forward.

One of the features of England's play during the 1966 World Cup was the link between Bobby Moore and his West Ham team-mate Geoff Hurst. Hurst worked hard and intelligently to free himself from marking and Moore reached him with accurate passes clipped forward from the left side of England's defence.

Leeds United, even when established as a force in European football, often chose to miss out their talented midfield players when playing out of defence in difficult away matches. Instead they hit long passes that their strikers were expected to hunt behind turning defenders.

If no chances are being made it is up to the more enlightened players to seek alternatives. Possession is fine but goals win matches.

Arthur Rowe's instruction to a famous Spurs team 25 years ago was 'Keep it simple, make it quick'. Times have changed. Defences are more difficult to break down. But it remains a sound principle.

Chapter Four
Heading

The classic comic book soccer hero rises to meet a centre from the wing and sends an unstoppable, cup-winning header past a helpless goalkeeper.

Soccer in reality thrives on such moments and the authors of its fiction are therefore right to select heading when attempting to emphasize the spectacular.

Heading represents the game's best features. Great headers of the ball are athletic, fearless, confident and skilful.

Size doesn't matter. Cliff Jones, Denis Law, Uwe Seeler and Pelé aren't tall men, but their headwork was devastating, while some tall players are criminally poor in the air. They time the ball badly and lack aggression and self-belief. Roberto Bettega (Juventus and Italy), Andy Gray (Aston Villa and Scotland), Joe Jordan (Manchester United and Scotland) and Kevin Keegan (Hamburg and England) stand out among contemporary players who head the ball well.

There is a basic heading technique. The ball should be struck with the middle of the forehead and the powerful neck muscles must be brought into play.

Once you have developed confidence – the forehead is made for heading – build up power.

Vary the services so that the player heading the ball will have to move backwards and forwards, timing his jump.

Getting to the ball is half the battle. Players who are outstanding in the air give the impression that they are 'hanging'. It is an illusion created by perfect timing. They are at the peak of their jump while others are either on the way down or still on the way

Basic heading technique. The ball is struck with the middle of the forehead and the powerful neck muscles are brought into play.

up. This sense of timing enables them to make maximum use of their upper body and the neck muscles, twisting from the waist to meet the ball full-on.

Defenders should not be content just to make contact when jumping to head. They must try to power the ball away from the danger zone. Gordon McQueen does this splendidly, sending the ball over great distances. But the ball may have to be cushioned as well as directed. Attackers who can do this are able to head the ball off accurately to supporting team-mates. Players worth watching for this ability are Brian Kidd (Manchester City), Joe Jordan (Manchester United), Paul Mariner and Trevor Whymark (Ipswich) and Frank Stapleton (Arsenal).

Remember, if you are heading for goal concentrate on accuracy. If you are heading out of defence, go for distance.

Always attack the ball. Be first. Be aggressive. Work at your jumping.

Far post headers

If Liverpool were to reach the 1978 European Cup Final they had to recover from a 2–1 defeat by Borussia Moenchengladbach in the first leg of the semi-finals.

It was a classic far post header by Ray Kennedy that brought them level on aggregate at Anfield, a seventh-minute goal that set up a memorable victory.

Kenny Dalglish, running smartly for a shrewd Souness pass, reached the goal-line and cut the ball back to the far side of Borussia's goal. Kennedy, with perfect timing, arrived at exactly the right moment to head a fine goal.

If he had gone in too early the centre would have gone over his head. If he had left his run too late Borussia's goalkeeper would have got the ball.

Even professionals are often guilty of moving in too soon when the ball is hit deep across goal from the opposite flank.

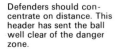

Defenders should concentrate on distance. This header has sent the ball well clear of the danger zone.

20

Attack the ball at all times. Getting there first is half the battle. Note how Clement has swivelled from the hips so that he makes contact with the front and not the side of his head.

Near post headers

Ron Greenwood was eager to introduce variety into England's attacking play when he took over as manager late in 1978.

He had appointed Geoff Hurst as one of his coaches and Hurst, when playing for Greenwood at West Ham, had perfected the art of heading goals from in front of the near post. Consequently, Hurst's demonstrations in those early coaching sessions were designed to show that it wasn't necessary to look for an attacker when crossing the ball to the near post. 'Just put the ball in' he said. 'I'll do the rest.'

If the attacker moves too early he will attract a marker in with him. By delaying his run the attacker gets the extra yard that may prove to be crucial.

Exercises

Practise heading in pairs standing, kneeling and sitting. Build up a

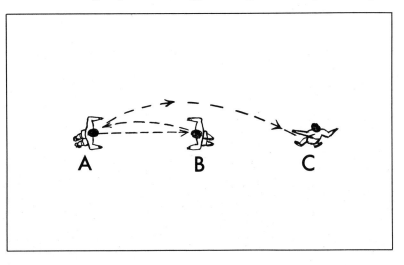

Diagram 3: B returns a header from A who heads to C.

Get used to challenging
for the ball in the air.

sequence. Stand and head. Kneel and head. Sit and head. Then
stand and head again.

Head in threes with one man in the middle.

Throw, head, catch Two teams play in a limited area. The first
pass is thrown to a team-mate who must head the ball, which can
be caught. The sequence must be maintained. The opposition can
intercept the throw or the header and build a sequence of their
own. Only headed goals count.

Head Tennis There are four, five or six a side. The teams are
restricted to a set number of touches on their side of the net. The
ball can be played with the feet or the head, but must be headed
over the net.

Chapter Five
Ball Control

'What about the big man' piped Archie Gemmill admiringly in a Rio hotel, interrupting the gentle rhythm that Martin Buchan had begun to pluck from a borrowed guitar. Scotland had just lost to Brazil in the summer of 1977 and a group of their players were relaxing as the South Atlantic hurried in splashing the windows with spray. 'Aye, what about the big man' smiled Danny McGrain, the fine Celtic full-back who was soon to suffer an injury that would keep him out of the 1978 World Cup.

They were talking about Luis Pereira, one of Brazil's central defenders. Examples of supreme skill are not uncommon in the Maracana stadium where vast crowds have thrilled over the years to the magic of Pelé, Garrincha, Didi, Tostao, Rivelino, Gerson and the rest, but even Brazilians familiar with such quality knew that Pereira, when repelling a Scottish attack, had shown them something special. Running full pelt towards his own goal and under pressure from Kenny Dalglish, the Brazilian hooked a bouncing ball back over his head, took it on his chest and then volleyed a perfect pass to Zico. It was an outstanding example of confident ball control, but McGrain, without attempting to de-value the skill, put it into professional perspective. 'What else could he do?' he asked innocently.

Absolute mastery of the ball is central to success in soccer. It will have to be controlled with the feet, the chest, the thighs and the head, mostly at speed and often under pressure.

Good ball control isn't an end in itself. You must put it to work.

Trapping with the sole of the foot.

23

Trapping on the volley with the inside of the foot. Remember to move towards the ball and to get away quickly.

Jugglers, masters of the ball but not of themselves, are of no use to the team.

Once the basics have been learned, the next aim should be swiftness. 'Attack' the ball, get to it quickly so that you gain time in which to take charge of the situation.

Do not practise ball control standing still. There are few opportunities to do this in a match. Unless you move off with the ball you are in danger of being tackled. Concentrate on reducing a series of movements to one. Get to the ball, control it and run without a noticeable break in rhythm.

As soccer speeds up, players get less time and there are fewer chances to control the ball with the feet. It is essential that you can control it with the chest, the thighs and the head.

Even in professional football, well-struck passes are wasted because of clumsy control. This won't happen if the receiving foot is drawn back at the moment of impact in the same way that the hands 'give' when catching a ball.

Trapping with the sole of the foot
When it is necessary to trap the ball dead it should be wedged

between the sole of the foot and the ground. If you bear down too heavily that's the last you will see of it for a while. 'He couldna trap a bag of cement' said Bill Shankly wickedly about a player who wasn't known for his ball control.

Well-balanced players make ball control look easy even when under immediate pressure. They position their bodies correctly and are able to make last minute adjustments. Roberto Rivelino (Brazil) is outstanding in this respect. He assesses things so quickly he is not only able to control the ball away from the threat of a tackle but in a direction that wrongfoots the defence.

By using the inside and outside of the foot you will be able to trap and turn. Make movement a habit. Feint to turn in one direction before controlling and turning the other way.

When facing your own goal with an opponent coming in from behind it is often wiser to pass back before sprinting for a return. But get used to controlling the ball under pressure, using your body as a 'screen'.

As long as you observe the law which prohibits use of the hands – unless of course you are a goalkeeper – it is unimportant how you control the ball, only that you receive it quickly, cleanly and comfortably. The Germans discovered that technically proficient players were less likely to tire on an uneven playing surface. Poor ball control uses up energy that could be directed elsewhere. Use the thighs to cushion passes that are too high to be controlled with the feet and too low for the chest.

Turning with the ball

If players always use the ball the way they are facing, teamwork will become predictable and as a result will be more easily contained. Turning with the ball is, nevertheless, a specialized skill that usually separates stars from average players.

Few players are good enough or brave enough to turn with the ball when they are being closely marked. But Mike Channon, Johan Cruyff, Kenny Dalglish, Trevor Francis, Steve Heighway, Sammy McIlroy, Rivelino, John Richards and Tony Woodcock

When screening the ball, keep it as far away as possible from the opponent.

A difficult pass well controlled with the thigh.

re good examples of players with this skill.

Nothing comes easy in a game so make things as difficult as possible when practising ball control. Get a partner to kick the ball high over your head. Turn, get beneath the ball and control it away to left or right. Work for skill at speed.

Working in pairs, smash the ball at each other from 20 to 25 yards. Move to the ball. Control it and return.

Some outstanding players have been conspicuously one-footed. Puskas did almost everything with his left foot and so does Norman Hunter, the Bristol City and former Leeds and England defender. But although most players favour one foot, this bias should not go unchecked. Don't ignore the weak foot when practising.

In the early stages it will be necessary to keep your eyes on the ball, but good players get their heads up quickly so that they can take in play.

Top: Forwards particularly must be able to screen the ball from a challenge when controlling it.

Above: A classic example of good ball control. The chest and inside of the foot have been used to receive and turn with the ball under pressure.

Chest control

Pelé when running at great speed could jump and take the ball on his chest, often deflecting it clear of a challenge and on into his stride. Few players will achieve that degree of skill, but chest control was a highly developed art in the 1978 World Cup.

To drop the ball at your feet, bring the shoulders forward and relax the chest at the moment of impact.

The chest can also be used as a platform on which the ball can be cushioned. What you are seeking here is a controlled rebound that will send the ball to left or right so that it can be passed on the volley or taken in mid-stride.

Time is at a premium and players cannot expect much of it. They must be able to cope with the ball when it is in the air and this is essential when ground conditions are poor.

Soft grounds are the rule rather than the exception in Britain and as a result the ball control of British players is often painfully inadequate on hard, uneven surfaces. It is partly because they are used to such conditions that South Americans generally show better ball control than most Europeans.

If it is a team policy to drive long passes forward to the strikers they will need men who can receive the ball at various heights and are able to bring the ball under control, shielding it from tackles until team-mates can hurry forward to support. Good examples are Stan Bowles (Queen's Park Rangers), Charlie George (Derby County), Stuart Pearson (Manchester United) and Frank Stapleton (Arsenal).

It is always fascinating to see a stage juggler cushion a ball with his head when it is thrown from the audience. There is not, in fact, a more delicate example of ball control and few footballers have mastered the art. Charlie Hurley, an outstanding Sunderland and Eire international centre-half, often intercepted long passes with his head, cushioning the ball before heading it forward beyond an advancing attacker. This skill demands a relaxing of neck muscles and perfect co-ordination. It's a long way down from the forehead to the feet so use the ball's pace as an ally.

First-time passing is football perfection. The best teams will produce it in short bursts and the skill involved will be beyond average players, so the ability to get the ball under control quickly, to receive it under pressure remains central to development.

Exercises

Ball control can be practised by driving the ball against a wall. Move to the ball. Control and turn. Repeat.

In small-sided games players must touch the ball only twice to control and then pass it.

Those players who have complete confidence in their technique can concentrate on other things. They will be able to take in a wider view of play and make their decisions more quickly.

Slack ball control not only disrupts teamwork but saps energy.

Chapter Six
Marking and Tackling

Marking

Helmut Schoen, then manager of West Germany, was criticized after the 1966 World Cup Final for using Franz Beckenbauer to mark Bobby Charlton. Charlton with his passing ability and immense shooting power was England's most feared attacker. Beckenbauer, then playing in midfield, was the most accomplished of the German players.

They both had an undistinguished game, but could Beckenbauer have contributed more to the German cause if he had been allowed to play more naturally? Schoen argued: 'Beckenbauer had the discipline to mark Charlton and equal skill on the ball if he won it from him.'

Beckenbauer was given the same job when England and West Germany met again in the World Cup four years later. This time it was a quarter-final in Leon, Mexico. Charlton was taken off 20 minutes from time with England leading 2–0. Beckenbauer, relieved of the responsibility, came forward and scored the goal which led to the Germans winning 3–2 in extra time. Such are the ironies of football.

The basic principle of marking is being goalside of your opponent, i.e. between him and the goal you are defending. Having got into this habit you should concentrate on staying in touch while being aware where the ball is.

Many defenders, even in top-class professional football, are guilty of what is known as 'ball watching'. They lose sight of the man they are responsible for and as a result are often caught out when he sneaks behind them or on the 'blind side'.

This is often evident in full-back play. When the defence is being attacked along one flank the full-back on the opposite side should position himself so that he can move in quickly to cover while at the same time keeping his man in view. If he is lured too far forward the ball may be flighted across to a player coming in around the back, but by taking a pace or two back towards his own goal the full-back can now attack the centred cross or turn to make contact with the player out wide.

Anxious or inexperienced defenders are often panicked into error by impatient spectators. They should try and resist the temptation to dive in when the odds aren't in their favour. Panic caused the West Germans to concede a first-minute penalty when playing Holland in the 1974 World Cup Final. The Germans had detailed Berti Vogts, an outstanding marker, to look after Johan Cruyff. Cruyff, picking the ball up in the centre of the field, outpaced Vogts and was brought down by Hoeness.

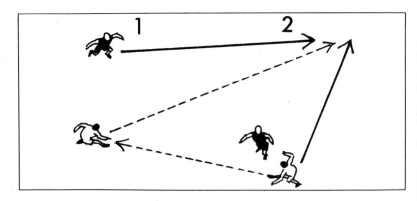

Defenders should always mark man-to-man close to their own goal, but should allow themselves a margin for error on the edge of the penalty area. The defender who gets too close may find himself stranded by a quick exchange of passes. Be close enough to prevent your man turning with the ball, but leave yourself room to adjust.

Thrusts through the middle appear to be most dangerous, but are they? The defence is usually strongest here and the ball angled to the flanks may be more threatening, particularly if it goes to a speedy, intelligent winger.

'Football is broken down into a series of duels between two men' says Ron Greenwood, the England manager. Kevin Keegan was completely aware of this after spending a season playing in West Germany, where man-to-man marking is a common practice. Once when training with the England team, Keegan was clearly using a six-a-side passing game as a marking practice and Greenwood pointed this out to him.

British defences still prefer to mark zones. This requires good mutual understanding, because attackers are shunted from one player to another. This requires good understanding.

It is worthwhile recalling Shankly's advice. 'Don't allow attackers to turn with the ball. Track them down quickly if they do.'

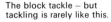

The block tackle – but tackling is rarely like this.

Tackling

Before the 1970 World Cup in Mexico and following controversial statements from Joao Saldanha, then the Brazilian team manager, Sir Alf Ramsey took a firm stand on what was for him a critical issue.

Back in Rio after a European tour, Saldanha made pointed references to brutal play. Ramsey, the England manager, insisted on fair play, but he defended the physical aspect of football because he felt it was essential. 'Tackling is important' he said. 'Without it we would be denying the public an exciting part of the game.'

Aggression and endeavour are admired. Players who drive in to win the ball fairly can expect as much applause as the ball artists.

Tackling is not mentioned in the laws of the game and there are various interpretations. The British version is based on the belief that it is legal to win the ball with a front-on or side-on challenge. As long as the tackler makes initial contact with the ball using a powerful thrust of the foot the tackle is adjudged to be fair, but this is not always acceptable elsewhere, particularly in South America.

Consequently it was feared that the 1970 World Cup in Mexico would be remembered mostly for violent attitudes, but the combination of altitude and heat reduced the momentum of play. Explosive moments were rare and firm refereeing in the opening game conditioned the teams to good behaviour.

Among the more stirring sights in that competition was a tackle by Bobby Moore, the England captain, on Brazil's swift and muscular winger, Jairzinho. Jairzinho, built like a well-trained middleweight, was a fearsome proposition in full flight and England's defence were entitled to feel nervous as he sped at them in Guadalajara. But the Brazilian found Moore in full command of the situation. There wasn't a hint of desperation – just perfect balance, immaculate timing and a powerful driving challenge that brought him clear with the ball. The crowd went silent. They had been shown what a good tackle was. Moore had rammed the skill down their throats.

There is no set technique. Old coaching manuals usually showed a picture of two players poised in identical posture over a static ball. Shoulders hunched forward, heads down, the tackling feet drawn back. This is the popular picture of what good tackling looks like.

Nothing is further from the truth. Good tacklers are simply those who consistently get possession, but there are essential factors common to all good ball-winners. They have the desire to win the ball against odds and they make full use of their strength. They are also brave.

'Tackling' said Wilf Copping, a famous old Arsenal and England wing-half 'is all to do with thinking you can. You don't have to be a giant to be a good tackler.' Nobby Stiles is slightly built, but there have been few better ball-winners than the former England and Manchester United World Cup star. Norman Hunter of Bristol City has an awesome reputation as a tackler and yet he is bony rather than big. 'Norman bites yer legs' warned the banners when Hunter played for Leeds.

Tackling was once left to the experts, to defenders who know their job. Now everyone is expected to tackle. Strikers must try and put defenders under pressure, working hard to prevent attacks being built from deep positions. The Dutch have proved that quick, collective tackling in midfield will discourage timid teams and disturb more stylish ones. Wingers who were once allowed to lurk on the touchlines waiting to be given the ball must now share the burden of defensive play getting back behind the ball when their team is being threatened.

Good tacklers keep their heads and stay on their feet although Dave Mackay was a classic exception to the rule. On a wet day he would tackle in a cloud of spray hurling himself recklessly at the ball, winning it consistently with a wide sweep. However, the sliding tackle is a desperate measure and should be kept for desperate situations, when it is impossible to shunt an opponent away from goal or when he may have built up enough speed to outstrip you along the touchline. Slide tackling in the penalty area is asking for trouble.

Knowing when to tackle is probably more important than knowing how to. This may not be as obvious in lower grades of football where the ball changes possession more frequently, but at professional level players must guard against over-commitment. Those who dive in regardless are usually left floundering.

Brave, confident forwards may even invite tackles and are perhaps less comfortable when being jockeyed into unfavourable situations.

Top-class teams such as Holland often tackle in clusters. If the first tackle has unbalanced the man on the ball, the second tackle usually counts.

Determined players will win the ball consistently, but determination alone is not enough. The good tackler is always watchful

and waits until he has a reasonable chance of success. When he strikes he strikes quickly. A desperate tackle, even if it works, is usually an indication of poor judgement and bad timing.

Forwards remember a good tackle. If they have been shaken up, they will be wary the next time and it can affect their confidence. Nothing upsets a skilful player more than to be tackled as he is trying to bring the ball under control.

To anticipate passes you must be able to sense what is coming next by watching the man on the ball and trying to judge where he intends to pass.

Jockeying

Life got tougher for Jimmy Greaves when defenders stopped lunging into tackles. A prodigious goalscorer, Greaves thrived on reckless attempts to stop his runs on goal. Sure-footed and quick, he could pick his way through a crowd of opponents. But techniques changed along with defensive systems; there was more concentration on containing play and jockeying forwards. 'Don't allow attackers to turn with the ball. Track them down quickly if they do' insisted Bill Shankly when discussing the basic principles of defensive play.

Get to know your opponents. A quick full-back can afford to mark his man closely because he has the speed to cope in a sprint. Never be flat-footed and if an attacker is approaching with the ball at speed be sideways-on so that you can adjust to a sudden change of pace. It is useless being yards away from a player who has run wide to collect a ball. Get in close and quickly otherwise he will be able to leave you in no man's land with a pass or a centre.

Most players favour one foot. Try to get them on their weak foot. In addition, watch for individual tricks. Good players may continue to make them work against you, but at least you shorten the odds.

Kevin Keegan, when with Liverpool, would feint to take the ball across his body to the left before flicking it the other way with the outside of his right foot. After a season with Hamburg in the Bundesliga, he was no longer using the trick as often, probably the result of close man-to-man marking.

It is difficult to practise tackling because realistic conditions are hard to create, but players can be encouraged to show more determination in small-sided games.

Exercises

Piggy in the Middle Six players pass the ball around a circle. Two players in the middle make determined attempts to win the ball and the players take it in turns to go into the middle.

Six-a-side Players must beat a man before passing.

Two-against-two Play in a small area.

Three-against-three The player with the ball must touch it at least six times before passing.

Chapter Seven
Running with and without the Ball

Running with the ball

David Fairclough's ability to come on and score important goals for Liverpool earned him the nickname 'Supersub'. It wasn't simply Fairclough's freshness that proved disconcerting to tiring defenders, but his direct approach to the game. He was eager to run at goal, trusting in his speed and determination in areas where most other players would be eager to pass.

Running with the ball as distinct from dribbling is a rare skill among British players although some have done it brilliantly. Think of Peter Barnes, George Best, Bobby Charlton, Charlie Cooke, Trevor Francis, Jimmy Greaves, Steve Heighway and Cliff Jones who all mastered a way of running with (or on) the ball so that it was always within playing distance. There should be no break in stride and the number of touches should be reduced to a minimum. By contrast, dribbling means constantly changing the direction and speed of the ball by quick touches with the feet.

Pelé watching the ball when running with the ball at his feet.

Where to run is equally important. The player who attacks an opponent head-on may get past, but he will not have disturbed the overall structure of the defence. A player like the Argentinian Kempes who attacks to left or right of an opponent will drag him to one side or the other and the defence will be forced to adjust, often in a panic.

Tony Woodcock was on loan to Doncaster Rovers when Nottingham Forest recalled him for a match at Millwall midway through the 1976–77 season. Woodcock kept his place. Forest gained promotion from the Second Division and easily won the First Division Championship at their first attempt. Woodcock had by then emerged as a player with an international future and won his first full cap for England against Northern Ireland at Wembley in May, 1978. He credited the Forest manager Brian Clough with the wisdom to offer him an entirely new conception of the game. 'Brian told me to take defenders on. To attack them with the ball. It made all the difference.'

Great runners with the ball acquire tricks that enable them to deceive opponents with sudden charges of pace. It may be possible to beat an opponent who dives in recklessly by pushing the ball past him on one side and collecting it on the other. Stopping and starting, i.e. checking the ball before accelerating, is another useful variation that will keep the opponents confused.

Players will soon tire if they are asked to sustain sprints with the ball. Practise in relays to create the added stimulus of competition. Use both feet. Play the ball with alternate feet.

Work for balance and use your body to try and wrongfoot defenders. Run with the ball, not after it.

Dribbling

Sir Stanley Matthews was for many years England's most famous footballer. Known as the 'Wizard of Dribble' he had uncanny close control and tremendous acceleration. He used his dribbling skills to get the full-back off-balance, his acceleration to burst clear and accurate passes pulled back from the goal line to make chances for the supporting strikers.

Dribbling can become self-indulgent. Tricks may appeal to the crowd, but do they lead to anything? Good dribbles are wasted if the final pass is poor, but the best dribbles can open up defences particularly along the flanks. Also remember that near your own goal a good pass is safer and better than a dribble.

It is difficult to eliminate Pelé and Alfredo di Stefano from any aspect of football technique. Both were great runners on the ball: Pelé more powerfully, di Stefano more studiedly. Pelé performed prodigious feats of control at speed and would deliberately knock the ball against an opponent's legs, taking the rebound in full stride. Controlling the ball at speed was also a characteristic of di Stefano, who could run with it and take part in any passing movement no matter how quickly the ball travelled.

Clement has unbalanced his opponent by swerving to his right and now accelerates swiftly.

Running without the ball

Teams who adopt predictable attacking formations, who continually plug the same avenue of approach, seldom if ever changing the pace of their play, are unlikely to make a lasting impression. The essence of top-class football is movement and imagination and the ability to react collectively to a sudden switch of initiative so that the opposition is continually threatened by unexpected thrusts at goal. If the players are willing to support the man on the ball intelligently, bravely and at speed, decisive raids can be made at the most vulnerable points.

Even in top-class football, forwards are guilty of 'marking' defenders, laying up against them, rarely moving off unexpectedly. Movement off the ball creates space, the extra ground that is invaluable when trying to escape close-marking or when attempting to leave holes that team-mates can fill. One of the reasons for Arsenal's defeat in the 1978 FA Cup Final against Ipswich was that strikers Macdonald and Stapleton were usually static, failing to provide options for passes from midfield.

Conversely one of the reasons for England's success in the 1966 World Cup was the intelligence and industry that Geoff Hurst and Roger Hunt brought to their task as front runners. Hurst and Hunt were always on the move, pulling defenders out of position, using the full width of the pitch, creating space that could be used by players hurrying forward from midfield.

Consider the situation where a player is advancing with the ball. As he moves forward he will be seeking to link up with the strikers, but if they anchor themselves on defenders, making no attempt to run them wide, he will be forced to travel on and accept the threat of a tackle. But once there is movement the whole picture changes. Perhaps someone will run wide. Someone else may be doubling back to invite a pass. Tostao ran off the ball brilliantly for Brazil in the 1970 World Cup. He would make sharp forward sprints before darting back to receive passes rolled in the space he had just left. So suddenly it's different. The defenders are on edge trying to reassess the situation, wondering where the threat will come from.

We talk about using the 'open space'. It's a loose phrase since space must be worked for. A player can run into space and achieve nothing simply because he has run offside. He will have done little better if his run leaves the defence still consolidated. The most productive runs are made into forward areas, preferably at an angle on the 'blind side' or behind defenders. Intelligent running is central to good team play, because it creates space that can be used by others.

Intelligent running by the front players will help to confuse defenders, particularly when it is synchronized with accurate passing. It will influence the type of attacks that can be attempted and the speed with which they can be mounted.

Mobility is a key factor in Holland's World Cup football as it has been in the play of their best club teams, Ajax, Feyenoord and PSV Eindhoven. Their defenders function brilliantly when running into attacking positions and this smooth interchange of responsibility has brought the Dutch many fine goals.

Many modern full-backs began their careers as wingmen and are therefore capable of taking full advantage of opportunities to move into attack. Remember that sharp decisive runs from the back will unnerve the opposition, whereas long, laboured runs are easily picked off.

Martin Peters might not have been 10 years ahead of his time as Sir Alf Ramsey once suggested, but there was no doubt that his game was marvellously modern. Peters' talent for 'stealing' into space is the product of vision and intelligence. If England's passing from midfield had been more perceptive, had they been able to recruit someone like Johnny Giles, to float the ball forward, there is no doubt that Peters would have scored many more goals for England.

Bobby Charlton with 49 goals remains England's record scorer and vividly recalls how a selfless run helped him to score one of them against Mexico in the 1966 World Cup. 'I had the ball on the halfway line and my first thought was to move it forward quickly. When I looked up Roger Hunt was streaming off on a cross-field run and half the Mexicans seemed to have gone with him. I just kept on running. When I got within range I was able to drive the ball into the far side of the goal. It was a great moment for me, but Roger deserved much of the credit.'

Good running from midfield can help to break down teams who push forward to compress the game into a narrow channel hoping to catch players offside. No-one did this better in England during the 1977–78 season than Terry McDermott of Liverpool. McDermott's reward should have come in the European Cup Final against Bruges, but when right through he struck his shot against the goalkeeper's legs.

Forwards should develop the habit of trying to find space for themselves and creating space for team-mates. That habit was built into Johan Cruyff at an early age. For the rest of his career he was conditioned to spurt forward before checking back to collect a pass. And once he had the ball his devastating speed and intelligent passes could destroy any defence.

Ferenc Puskas was another who knew the value of finding space when off the ball. Maurice Setters, a former Manchester United captain, recalls playing against Puskas when the great Hungarian was still appearing for Real Madrid as a veteran. 'I was marking Gento who had the ball at his feet. Puskas came square offering himself for a square pass. Gento ignored him. Puskas then sprinted into a forward position. Gento ignored him again. So Puskas checked and came back square. He must have covered 200 yards without getting the ball and in the playing sense he was an old man.'

Chapter Eight
Restarts

Liverpool goalkeeper Ray Clemence was held responsible when West Germany scored from a crucial free-kick against England early in 1978. England, reviving under their new manager Ron Greenwood, were a goal in front and carrying the game to the then World Champions when they conceded a free kick just outside the penalty area. The Germans used a succession of deceptive ploys to unsettle the English defenders and when the shot came it went between Clemence and his near post. It emphasized not only the need to be fully aware of what opponents may attempt but the value of initiative.

Free kicks, corners and throw-ins are frequent and they offer teams the opportunity to demonstrate their imagination. It is worth remembering, after all, that almost a third of the goals scored in an English First Division season come from free kicks and corners.

The ability to 'bend' and 'dip' the ball is invaluable and players with this special skill should be encouraged to use it.

Simplicity should be the prime consideration whether planning to make the most of the kick-off or a throw-in on the halfway line; complicated moves are more likely to break down and the free kick that flies directly into goal cannot be improved upon.

A free kick within striking distance of goal will usually be opposed by a 'wall' of opponents, usually midfield men and forwards with regular defenders concentrating on marking.

The wall should be set so that it covers the space between the middle of the goal and the near post, protecting the goalkeeper from a direct shot. Goalkeepers in amateur or junior football may scorn the wall, demanding that they be allowed to see the shot from the moment it is struck. This is fatal at professional level where the ball is clubbed with such force that the goalkeeper is likely to be beaten by sheer pace.

If the wall is positioned correctly – this can be the responsibility of the goalkeeper or an outfield player who lines the wall up from behind the ball – it will be difficult to score with a direct shot. It then becomes necessary to work out moves to produce an on-target shot, especially if there is someone skilled at swerving the ball. Deception is important if defenders are to be lured into false positions. Decoy running, calling and general movement will cause confusion and increase the chance of success. The ball lifted over the wall for an attacker running in at an angle and the one played wide for someone else are simple, thoughtful free kicks.

Leeds for all their planning and experience were beaten by a simple move when playing Barcelona at Elland Road in the first

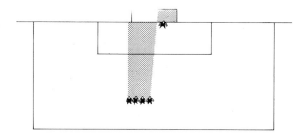

Diagram 5: The correct method of setting the wall of players to help protect the goal at free kicks. The wall should overlap the near post by one player so that the ball cannot be swerved around that side. The wall covers the near side of the goal. The goalkeeper concentrates on covering shots into the far side.

leg of the 1975 European Cup semi-finals. Johan Cruyff passed the ball square across the Leeds wall by-passing the nearest Barcelona player, but directly into the path of another. Leeds, plunging at the threat, made desperate attempts to narrow the angle, but the shot flew through them and found the corner of the goal.

Professional teams, wary of the swerved shot, set the wall so that it overlaps the near post by one player. The wall should never break and one man should be stationed on the end nearest the centre of the goal, ready to thrust forward and challenge.

Play to strength. Players who shoot powerfully and can swerve the ball should be given the chance to do so. Power shooting may unnerve the opposition and perhaps someone will duck.

A man with the ability to hurl the ball a long way creates problems, because a throw-in can then be as valuable as a corner. Ian Hutchinson, a Chelsea striker whose career was prematurely ended by injury, and Martin Chivers, a former England forward, made maximum use of this technique. Powerful men, they could reach the penalty spot with throws and this gave opposing defences, particularly if vulnerable in the air, an added problem.

The throw-in. Observe the laws and practise for accuracy.

Players with this exceptional skill are often wasted because of poor positioning in the goalmouth. It would take an extremely strong man to equal kicking power with his arms and even though he may be able to flight the ball into the danger area it rarely arrives with much power.

Individual talent should be taken into account. A brave player with outstanding heading ability can, for instance, sprint to meet the ball, glancing it back or turning it on in front of the other attackers. Hutchinson's throws were consistently dangerous because he learned to vary the trajectory, sometimes throwing long, low balls from the halfway line.

The throw-in taken quickly by the nearest man to the ball will often pay off. The opposition have little time to mark attackers and a few seconds start can be critical.

It is criminal to lose possession at a throw-in, worse if possession is lost close to your own goal. Never throw the ball square across field when you are deep in your own half.

Don't crowd the thrower unless there is a pre-arranged plan to by-pass the group who are attracting opponents in with them. Players who stand too close to the thrower will restrict movement and cut down on the space that can be used.

Take the example of a player throwing-in from a point 20 yards inside his own half of the field. His full-back will generally be free, but if the full-back comes too close he cuts down on the time and space he can make use of if the ball comes to him. By keeping his distance he creates this space.

Anyone can take a throw-in. But can they? Throw-ins break down, even at professional level, because of inaccuracy.

Things to remember
Don't make life difficult for the receiver. Make sure that he gets the ball where it can be controlled comfortably.

Don't throw to players who are tightly marked if they lack the skill to cope.

Don't be predictable. Vary the throw-ins. On the other hand, keep your moves simple.

Crowd the opposition, especially if they are trying to build a move with a throw-in from their own half of the field, and when you have ample players in the immediate area of the ball.

If you have an abundance of tall players use them. Call them up into the penalty area for free kicks and corners. They will have to be marked and that will be difficult. Short corners may work and are useful as a variation to long corners. They will also lure defenders out of the penalty area.

Use your most accurate kickers, players who are able to pin-point the ball, swinging it in or out, driving it deep to the far side of goal or dropping it in short.

Crowded penalty areas and the presence of tall attackers make life hard for the goalkeeper and he will often struggle to catch or punch. But he is the boss and should be given every opportunity to attack the ball. This means making sure that he is covered, certainly on the post nearest the point of attack.

Tall forwards are usually detailed to mark defenders who have moved up for free kicks and corners. But the most dangerous opponent should be taken by a defender who is capable of dealing with him in the air.

Jack Charlton, the former Leeds and England centre-half, always positioned himself wide of the goal area, so that he could defend against the high centre. Half a yard is all that an attacker needs to meet the ball with a scoring header. The defender who starts late will usually finish second.

Penalty kicks

Penalty kicks are a matter for the individual. They can be smashed, stroked or curled. All that matters is that they go in.

When selecting a penalty kicker go for accuracy and nerve. The straightest kicker, the coolest head.

The odds are against the goalkeeper with a penalty. Even if he guesses right, a confident penalty taker will usually beat him.

Chapter Nine
Goalkeeping

One of football's rare tragedies occurred in the 1930s when Johnny Thomson, a brilliant young Glasgow Celtic goalkeeper, died after making a save against Glasgow Rangers. Thomson was only 21 years old and already established in Scotland's team when he attempted to take the ball from the feet of the Rangers forward, Sam English. English was unable to pull up in time, and Thomson took a blow on the head. It was a pure accident, but Thomson died in hospital.

In the 1956 FA Cup Final, Bert Trautmann, a former German paratrooper who had been a prisoner of war in England, came close to suffering a similar fate when he hurled himself at the feet of a Birmingham forward, Peter Murphy. Trautmann clutched the ball to his chest, but Murphy had no chance to avoid a collision with the big German. His knee cracked violently but accidentally against Trautmann's neck.

After treatment the German carried on, although he could hardly stand. City won that Final, but in the dressing room afterwards it was discovered that Trautmann had played through the final phase of the game with his neck broken.

Goalkeepers have always had to accept such perils and it has inspired the suggestion that most of them are crazy. Why else would they do the job?

Those who do it brilliantly are worth 12 points a season to a First Division club as Brian Clough, the Nottingham Forest manager, stressed when paying Stoke a huge fee for Peter Shilton in 1977. Forest went on to win the League Championship and there were many matches when Shilton looked and proved unbeatable.

Ironically, Shilton had been bought by Stoke to replace Gordon Banks, the great goalkeeper he had understudied as a boy at Leicester.

Banks, before suffering a serious eye injury, set standards of agility, courage and judgement that few have matched and when saving from Pelé in the 1970 Mexico World Cup was credited with the greatest save of all time.

It was a centre from the right that gave the great Brazilian a chance to head powerfully from above Alan Mullery's attempted challenge and Pelé admitted later that he had never felt more certain about scoring. But Banks, diving backwards, scooped the ball over the bar with the inside of his right wrist and Pelé clutched his head in disbelief. It not only emphasized the extent of Banks' brilliance but the confidence that an outstanding goalkeeper brings to a team.

The goalkeeper, in fact, is the most important individual in the team. If he plays well as Shilton did for Nottingham Forest in the 1977–78 season he gives his team-mates a tremendous boost. If he plays badly the team will probably lose.

Goalkeepers must concentrate all the time and particularly when the opposition is inferior. If the goalkeeper relaxes, a sudden breakaway can ruin an hour of good work by the team if he fails to react promptly to the threat.

The goalkeeper needs to practise as much as the other players, but he should not offer himself simply as a target in shooting practices. He is the only player who is allowed to use his hands and should work towards perfection when catching, handling and gathering the ball.

A good goalkeeper should be able to spring beyond the full length of his body when lying prone with arms outstretched. He must have a knowledge of angles and know when to leave his goal in order to intercept long through passes.

Below left: Gathering a ball along the ground.

Below right: Dealing with a ball at head height.

He must be able to cope with the unexpected. Deflections, miskicks and rebounds. It calls for sharp reflexes, gymnastic ability and speed. The goalkeeper ideally should be the quickest player in the team.

Handling and catching are the priorities for a goalkeeper. He should practise these all the time, building up strength in his wrists and hands to deal with the most powerful shots. If possible goal-keepers should work together, although by playing in outfield positions during practice games they may get a better appreciation of the problems that confront the other players.

Basic techniques for handling and catching a ball

Ball along the ground The body and hands should be behind the ball both when standing or kneeling. The little fingers should be touching when holding the ball. Get the ball up to the chest as quickly as possible.

Ball at head height Cushion the ball with your hands. Don't let it hit your hands. Bring the ball down to the chest quickly.

Catching Crosses are a constant problem for goalkeepers. School-boy players get little practice because few youngsters can centre the ball. Professionals on the other hand will be bombarded with centres if there is the slightest suggestion of a weakness in dealing with them. A high cross into a crowded goal area is especially dangerous. Look for the point in the air where you can get to the ball above everyone. Select a path that will get you in position. Be decisive. Catch when you can but, whether catching or punching, go all the way.

Be aggressive. Forwards will often be wary of challenging an aggressive keeper. Let your own players know that you are going for the ball. Don't be afraid of knocking them out of the way.

Positioning Favour the far post for a cross, it is easier to go forwards than backwards. If the attacker chooses to cut in then move towards the near post either to guard against a shot or to narrow the angle.

Punching Only punch when it is impossible to catch. Pat Jennings, the Arsenal and Northern Ireland goalkeeper, has huge hands and is an outstanding catcher but says: 'There are so many players in the penalty area at corners these days it isn't easy to get to the ball. I don't like punching, but there are times when I have to. Whether you use two hands or one make sure you punch the ball as far from goal as possible.'

The goalkeeper has to recover and get back after punching. A weak punch may leave him vulnerable to a chip or a lob.

Palming over the bar A centre close to the crossbar presents a special problem. Catching or punching may be difficult and dangerous. Palm the ball over.

Diving to save Holland might easily have won the 1978 World Cup if Rensenbrink's powerful drive in the first half hadn't been marvellously saved by the Argentinian goalkeeper Fillol.

Fillol not only had the spring to hurl himself left and upwards into the line of shot, but the strength in his hand to divert the ball for a corner.

It isn't enough to reach the ball, especially if there are alert attackers following up. The ball must be turned behind for a corner or forced as far from goal as possible.

Narrowing the angle Knowing when and when not to come out is always a problem for young goalkeepers and good judgement in this respect often influences selection at international level.

There was nothing to choose between Ray Clemence of Liverpool and Peter Shilton of Nottingham Forest when they were both included in the England squad, but Clemence kept the job because he was better at coming out to deal with through passes.

The goalkeeper should try and force the attacker to shoot at the least favourable angle. This means persuading him to shoot at the point which suits the goalkeeper best. Show him one side, an

uneven view of the goal, and be ready to leap into the larger gap — and stand up! A goalkeeper who stands right up to an attacker often terrifies him. He may panic and shoot wide, so make yourself look as large as possible.

Diving at a forward's feet Shots that hit a goalkeeper's legs bring groans of anguish from thwarted forwards and fans, but what may look like good fortune is usually expert goalkeeping.

It isn't simply to avoid injury that professional goalkeepers don't plunge headfirst at an attacker. They throw themselves sideways to present the widest possible barrier. If you get the ball then

Above: If in doubt, punch — but make the punch count.

Far left: Be safe. A dropping ball can be tipped safely over the bar.

Left: The same tipping-over technique used for a high centre.

49

Above left: The goal-keeper uses his full length to make life difficult for the attacker. Never dive headfirst at the forward's feet.

Above right: The long punt often unsettles the opposition.

hang on to it, hugging it into your chest. If the ball runs loose then fight for it!

Diving to cut out a low cross This requires courage and perfect timing. Work out the flight and then attack the ball! If you have gone to the near post the ball may be pulled back at too wide an angle for you to get there. By staying on your line you still have a chance of dealing with a shot if it comes.

Distribution Throwing is more accurate, but the opposition may take advantage if it is standard practice. They may crowd in and it will then become difficult to move the ball. Only throw to

Above left: Switching play with a one-handed throw.

Above right: Throwing for distance. Some goalkeepers can almost reach the halfway line.

unmarked players and never to those who are in danger of being dispossessed if they turn.

The ball should be thrown quickly. Delay usually means that there are no unmarked players left. The best throws go to the wings and to the opposite flank from which the ball has been collected.

All goalkeepers should be able to kick a long way. They should be able to kick a dead ball and punt out of their hands. Jim Standen, West Ham's goalkeeper when they won the European Cup Winners Cup in 1965, kicked wonderfully accurate half volleys that started many attacks. It is a rare skill. Goalkeepers should get as much kicking practice as possible.

Teamwork

Silent goalkeepers are a problem. They confuse their fellow defenders and can't 'boss' the penalty area as they should. Listen to the top men who are always shouting, calling, demanding, advising, bringing decision to their domain.

Exercises

To improve reflexes Instead of facing the ball, stand on the goal line with your back to the pitch. When you hear a shout turn and deal with shots or throws.

To improve spring power Kneel on the ground and attempt to save half-hit shots.

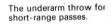
The underarm throw for short-range passes.

Chapter Ten
Systems and Tactics

Herbert Chapman, Nereo Rocco and Sir Alf Ramsey probably did most to influence systems of play.

Malcolm Allison, a highly successful coach and manager said this: 'Chapman with the introduction of the third back game when with Arsenal in the 1930s, hit upon something that lasted for 20 years. Rocco perfected the defensive tactics which became the basis of Italian play and that of many other countries throughout the world. Sir Alf Ramsey won the First Division Championship with Ipswich Town and the World Cup for England by a revolutionary new way of arranging the team.'

Ramsey's 'arrangements' had far-reaching effects throughout British football. Inheriting from Walter Winterbottom a 4-2-4 system, he reluctantly abandoned it because he could not find the players to make it work for him. His compromise, a variety of 4-3-3, won England the World Cup, and four years later a further revision of ideas led to the Cup being defended by a team playing 4-4-2.

When Ramsey entered management in 1955 at Ipswich there were others planning new strategies. In South America the Brazilians, hurt by a violent failure in the 1954 World Cup, were leading the race.

In winning the World Cup in Sweden in 1958, Brazil demonstrated to the world the value of integrating team play and of deploying four defenders in a line across the width of the field. By the time Brazil triumphed in Sweden other countries' full-backs were beginning to position themselves alongside opposing wingers, so denying them the opportunity of receiving the ball in space. The two central defenders provided cover for each other in the middle of the defence.

Brazil still used four attackers with two men 'feeding' them from midfield, but early pressure by Sweden in the 1958 Final forced the Brazilian left winger Zagalo to drop deep. Thus what had been 4-2-4 became for a while 4-3-3 and there was the first clue to a new system.

The experience was to have a profound effect on Zagalo who later managed the Brazilian teams of 1970 and 1974. He replaced the more romantic Saldanha with Brazil's preparation well under way and immediately set about organizing his defence.

Brazil in Mexico were credited with using two wingers and the adventurous system of 4-2-4. They played, in fact, as they had done in the initial stages of the 1958 Final. Zagalo confirmed this saying: 'When England lost narrowly in Rio in 1969 it was obvious that we would run into problems if we persisted in using two men

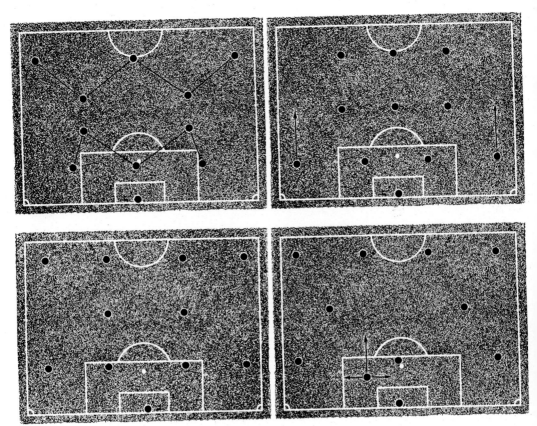

Top left: **Diagram 6:**
The WM formation.

Top right: **Diagram 7:**
The 4–3–3 formation.

Bottom left: **Diagram 8:**
The 4–2–4 formation.

Bottom right: **Diagram 9:**
Man-to-man marking
against a 4–3–3
formation with one other
defender playing as a
sweeper.

in the middle of the field. England only lost that night because they ran out of steam at the end of a difficult tour. They outnumbered us in the middle of the field and it was hard for our players. In Mexico we settled for a similar system with Rivelino operating from midfield on the left and Pelé playing in the manner of Bobby Charlton. Tostao and Jairzinho were our front men. Our advantage was that we had more expressive players and that we were better at altering the rhythm of a game. But England were the best team we met. I should not have liked to have played them in the Final.'

When Ramsey took over from Walter Winterbottom in 1963 he inherited a 4-2-4 formation. It had worked reasonably well for England but not well enough. Ramsey, nevertheless, began by experimenting with wingers and they were still appearing in his teams as late as 1965. But in December of that year following an unimpressive run he used three players in the middle of the field against Spain in Madrid.

A system is useless unless it can be effectively operated by the players who are available. It is the players who must come first. What Ramsey wanted was a system that best suited the qualities evident in the English player. It needed to encompass skill, high morale, fitness and strength. He settled on 4-3-3.

The complement of the team was not decided until fairly late when Jack Charlton emerged at last as a responsible player to complete a back four of Cohen, Charlton, Moore and Wilson.

It was the selection in midfield that aroused most controversy as England approached the World Cup. The three players deployed in the middle of the field had to have a balance of discipline and flair. Nobby Stiles, competitive and with infectious enthusiasm, got the job of covering across the front of the defence . . . Martin Peters was brought in to play on the left. Bobby Charlton, previously used as a left winger, was shrewdly switched to direct operations. Charlton was now able to use his enchanting ability to hit sweeping forward passes to the front men. Retreating defences gave him the space to move forward and use his powerful shooting.

With Alan Ball running endlessly on the right, the pattern was completed by Roger Hunt and Geoff Hurst who had the willingness and intelligence to enable Ramsey to alter the concept of forward play. Instead of playing in channels up and down the pitch forwards had to move sideways – the absence of wingers gave Hunt and Hurst the space to do so.

Another aspect of Ramsey's faith in 'all purpose' players was the encouragement he gave to his full-backs. Cohen and Wilson were also ordered to use the space vacated by the now absent wingers.

Amendments were made in 1970 because of special problems presented by altitude and heat in Mexico. Here Ramsey used four midfield men more obviously than he had done in 1966.

By 1973 he had not only settled for three attackers again but had begun to think seriously about the system used successfully by West Germany.

The Germans, with strict man-to-man marking and a superb covering defender in Franz Beckenbauer, overcame England in the 1972 European Championship and were handsome winners of the tournament. It was the system designed by Nereo Rocco and Ramsey liked it, but his fate was settled when England failed to qualify for the 1974 World Cup.

One game later against Italy at Wembley he switched to man-to-man marking. Italy won 1–0. Ramsey was manager for one more game – a 0–0 score against Portugal in Lisbon.

An unemotional man, unpopular with the media, Ramsey had an unbreakable bond with his players. He also made people think about team play and how it could be related to special individual skills.

The system that had begun to interest him helped to win the World Cup for West Germany in 1974 and England were still playing 4-3-3 a year after Don Revie took the team over.

Revie's quest was for more expression in midfield and better finishing. But Revie, like Ramsey in the latter stages of his reign, was short of talented players. England failed to qualify for the finals of the European Nations Championship and by the summer of 1977 it was clear that they were unlikely to reach the 1978

World Cup in Argentina.

Meanwhile the Dutch and the Germans continued to dominate Europe with a fluid system of play that blended outstanding technique with athleticism. Beckenbauer's influence on the German team was enormous as he used the space at the rear of his defence to mastermind attacks with precision passing and controlled sorties up field. Revie, disenchanted and keen to secure his future, resigned in the summer of 1977 after signing a contract with the United Arab Emirates.

The job of leading England out of the wilderness went to Ron Greenwood, who had established an international reputation when managing West Ham. Greenwood, wrongly labelled a theorist, was determined to broaden the scope of English football. He brought in players who could function wide on the flanks as wingers of the past once did.

But Greenwood, when in Argentina for the 1978 World Cup, sensed that radical changes were necessary back home. He too favoured a switch to a system that would accommodate man-to-man marking, but knew that it would be pointless unless the English clubs adopted it wholesale.

He also saw Scotland's passionate assault collapse in shame and scandal at Cordoba where they were also victims of a naive tactical policy.

Despite his experience in South America the previous summer Ally MacLeod, the Scottish manager, failed to recognize the the dangers of trying to defend on the edge of the penalty area against South American teams, and his team fell to Peru in the opening game. A draw against Iran was the next blow and it wasn't until the final game against Holland that the Scots settled for the strategy that might have made so much difference to their cause. They brought in Graham Souness to make a fourth man in mid-field and abandoned the policy of playing with a winger. The result; a 3–2 win that recalled Scotland's original potential.

It proved that it is players who matter and that tactics and systems must be suited to their ability. The coach should ask: 'Which formation is best for the men I have available?' and work from there.

English league club managers continually complain that school-boys know more about formations and tactics than they do about the application of skill. Ted Bates, a former manager of Southampton, said: 'These kids learn about winning before they learn how to play.'

The important thing at junior level is that players learn about teamwork and compactness, the need for width and depth both in defence and attack.

The pressures in professional football can be quite fearsome and as a result there is a tendency towards defensive play. Fear, bad coaching and the impossible attitudes of directors who refuse to see that only a handful of teams can succeed each season influence

ie state of the game. As a result the public have to suffer long
eriods of negative football.

This should not happen lower down the scale where there is less
eed to play defensively. There is rarely a large crowd and little
dvantage in playing at home. There will be more errors, the ball
ill change hands more often and therefore the team that attacks
iore effectively is likely to win.

Don't get bogged down with systems, but try to build a balanced
eam that can be taught to understand the fundamental principles
f play, most critically a sensible balance between attack and
efence. Ensure that you have cover in defence, that there is an
ffective linking force in midfield and that attacks are well
upported. Experiment by all means, but leave the heavy stuff to
ie professionals.

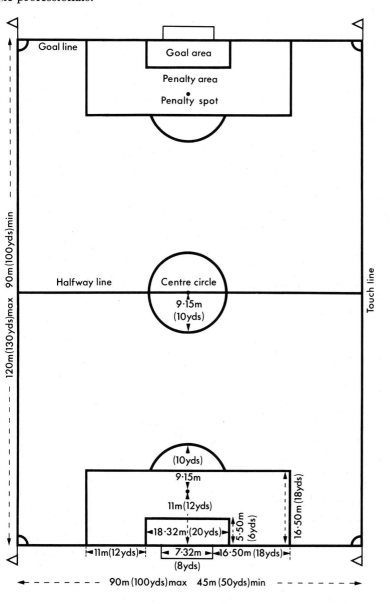

Diagram 10: The
dimensions of a soccer
pitch.

Chapter Eleven
Assessing the Play

Tears flowed at Wembley on May 29, 1968 when Manchester United at last won the European Cup. The years of striving, the residual grief for a previous team destroyed in a plane crash at Munich and the affection for their manager Matt Busby merged into a great wave of emotion. Three goals in the opening 10 minutes of extra-time finished off Benfica. The triumph was complete.

Yet there had been a moment in the second half when Busby's dream might have been shattered if Eusebio had kept his head. A supreme individualist and the most powerful shot in the world, he suddenly pierced United's defence with a sprint through the middle. Goalkeeper Alex Stepney advanced smartly from his line, but the odds were heavily in favour of the black Portuguese star. Eusebio shot, Stepney saved and the famous stadium shivered with relief. It was still 1–1.

But Busby knew that United had benefited not only from Stepney's alert play, but also from Eusebio's refusal to settle for the simple thing. Recalling that moment 10 years later Busby said 'I thought it was all over. If Eusebio hadn't tried to burst the net, if he'd just stuck the ball away as he should have done, then we wouldn't have won.'

Only a handful of spectators realized the extent of Eusebio's blunder, which helps to prove that professionals watch a different game. Fans follow the ball. Professionals follow the play.

For the professionals the vast majority of goals are conceded because at some point in the build-up of the move, some player has not done his job; only a small percentage are dismissed with a shrug of the shoulders as unstoppable, as entirely due to the skill of the opposition.

For the spectator the standards of examination need not be so harsh, but it is worth borrowing some of the judgement of the professionals before applying the label 'great' or 'magnificent'.

Many significant goals – or in Stepney's case, saves – owe as much, if not more, to shortcomings in application as to brilliant technique.

Managers and coaches must try to remain detached however tense the circumstances. Only then will they be able to pinpoint the critical factors emerging from the match. It is not enough, for instance, to accept that an individual is having an 'off' day. If the player is working hard, still inviting the ball, then the reasons for his apparent poor form might be found elsewhere. Is he being singled out for special attention by the opposition? Is he suffering because team mates are not taking up good positions? Is he having o accept too much responsibility when attempting to contain play?

Some players cheat. They appear to be working hard when they are not. They do their running when it doesn't matter. They play safe. Others are forced to accept the burden. Experienced observers will not be fooled. The game they see will differ from the one that will be discussed by the fans.

While the spectators are warming to the mood of a match, professionals will have already begun to form an objective analysis. They start by noting the tactical arrangement of the teams. Do the defenders mark zones or do they follow a man-to-man marking system? How many players are being used in midfield and which of them are responsible for going forward? Do the defences retreat or are they more likely to try to compress the game into the middle of the field?

As a pattern of play emerges it may be obvious that one of the teams is dominating. What are the reasons for this? They may be physically stronger and more competitive. They may be benefiting from slack play by their opponents. Are they taking maximum advantage of their domination? If not why not? Liverpool threatened to overwhelm Nottingham Forest in the League Cup final at Wembley in March, 1978, but failed to score. The principal fault lay with their finishing. Chances were made and squandered. This may not have been simply the result of deficient technique. It could be that the attackers were unwilling to accept the responsibility for putting the ball into the net.

Leeds when losing to Bayern Munich in the 1975 European Cup final were faulted by neutral observers for relying almost exclusively on high ball attacks. 'They had no variation' said Ferenc Puskas, the former Real Madrid star.

Variation is a thing to look for. Do attacks develop along the same lines or are attempts being made to introduce surprise? Does the attack have width? Are there wingers? If the wingers are being used, do they play intelligently? Some teams by tradition prefer to build their game from defensive positions and Spurs under Bill Nicholson were a good example. If this is so then it is worth noting whether attackers are willing to pressurize the build-up.

What happened to Holland's glowing football when they lost to West Germany in the 1974 World Cup Final?

They reached Munich on a fanfare of open play that had carried them convincingly through the group matches. But an early penalty goal after the Dutch forward Cruyff had been brought down entirely altered the mood of their game. They became cautious and the Germans were encouraged to stage a come-back. The order to take advantage of the respite came from the German coaches.

The most important moment in play comes when the ball is won or given away. Being able to take advantage of this switch of initiative will often determine the result of a match. Rapid collective reaction may produce a decisive attack.

Bayern Munich were under enormous pressure in the 1975 European Cup Final, but broke away to score two fine goals. On each occasion the attack was supported at speed and in enough strength to panic Leeds into error.

So which players concentrate fully for the whole match? Looking back on that European Cup Final Terry Yorath said: 'When you are under constant pressure it is easier to get things right. You get into a groove. But when you have as much of the ball as we did against Bayern there is always the danger of slackness. You get a little casual. You get caught out like we did.'

Defenders need to work well together, particularly when they are passing attackers from one zone to another. The two central defenders in such a system must have a good understanding as should the midfield players.

A team that continually gets stretched cannot hope to succeed. Why is it being stretched?

Is it because defenders aren't supporting the play closely enough? Do the defenders retreat too soon and too quickly? Do the attackers run too far ahead of the man in possession?

Patience is necessary in top-class football. In recent years it has been one of Liverpool's main virtues. Many of their victories have been won late in a game following long periods of relentless pressure.

Inexperienced teams are usually impatient. They are either under pressure or applying it.

The average spectator is largely impatient. He demands end-to-end play with its higher proportion of incident.

Professionals admire teams who have the confidence to pace their game with periods of possession football.

The strengths and weaknesses of individual players will be known in professional football. Expressive players may appeal to the crowd, but are they making a practical contribution to the team effort? A successful dribbler looks good, but is he upsetting team rhythm?

Long square passes are useful as a means of changing play, but rarely deserve the applause they get. The best passes eliminate defenders, but they aren't always on target. They may also be ruined by lack of effort further forward.

It isn't difficult for an experienced professional to 'lose' himself if things are going badly. The honest player continues to seek the ball and to use it productively even when well below form. The fact that he will almost certainly be barracked by spectators emphasizes the difference between amateur and professional viewing.

ndex